Nidhi was born and grew up in the bustling and vibrant city that is Manchester. She is currently a medical student and has always had a passion for writing and immersive poetry. In this book, Nidhi shares an in-depth insight into love whilst also exploring the feelings of pain felt when this is lost. She highlights the true role time plays in offering peace, helping with self-love, and healing.

The greatest kindness you can show to yourself, is embracing the freedom of finally letting go.

Nidhi Bhat

The Beauty in Broken

AUSTIN MACAULEY PUBLISHERS

LONDON • CAMBRIDGE • NEW YORK • SHARJAH

Copyright © Nidhi Bhat 2024

The right of Nidhi Bhat to be identified as author of this work has been asserted by the author in accordance with sections 77 and 78 of the Copyright, Designs and Patents Act 1988.

All rights reserved. No part of this publication may be reproduced, stored in a retrieval system, or transmitted in any form or by any means, electronic, mechanical, photocopying, recording, or otherwise, without the prior permission of the publishers.

Any person who commits any unauthorised act in relation to this publication may be liable to criminal prosecution and civil claims for damages.

A CIP catalogue record for this title is available from the British Library.

ISBN 9781398485044 (Paperback)
ISBN 9781398485051 (ePub e-book)

www.austinmacauley.com

First Published 2024
Austin Macauley Publishers Ltd®
1 Canada Square
Canary Wharf
London
E14 5AA

I want to thank my Mum and my Dad, for all their love and infinite support throughout my life. I would not be the person I am today without them. I would also like to thank all my beautiful friends for all their unconditional support and limitless love.

I am forever grateful to have such amazing people in my life and I would like to take this opportunity say that I love you all of you endlessly.

Table of Contents

Heads or Tails	11
You Said Forever	12
Lost	14
If Only She Knew	15
Bad Habits	16
Like Lovers Do	17
Joker	18
Happy to See Me Hurting	19
Invisible	20
Is That You?	21
Fading	22
Sweet Surrender	24
It Was Too Late	25
Was It Real?	26
This Pain	27
Stunted-Growth (I)	28

Self-Growth (II)	29
Tongue-Tied	30
50/50	31
No Caller ID	32
Plot-Twist	33
Our Last Hello	34
It Hurt Me, to Hold On	35
Two Hearts	36
Act of Kindness	37
Out of Touch	38
Other Side	39
All I Have Left	40
Love to Hate	41
Your Name	42
When the Sky Is Grey	43
Progress, Not Perfection	44
Tidal	45
Protect Your Peace	46
Too Comfortable	47
She Is Art	48
Time-Lapse	49
Drifting	50
Note to Self	51

Daydreams	52
Boundaries	53
The Healing	54
For the First Time	55
In This Moment	56
Her Vibe	57
Sunrise	58
Wishing You Well	59

Heads or Tails

The game of deceit,
is one that you had mastered so well.
The skill with which you deflected
any blame for your faults, intrinsic.
The waves of love and concern
just an intricate façade,
behind which, lay a maze of lies.

You controlled the chances,
no matter which way the disarray was flipped,
the odds would always stand with you.
My ache, my pain, my side
would never be seen.

In this game of heads or tails
you played with a weighted coin,
knowing you would always win.

You Said Forever

I remember only smiling, when you were around,
the mention of your name, ignited
a warm glow within me,
my sanctuary in you.
But then – I remember the cracks and the tears,
the way I was made to look stupid,
simply for loving you.
My friends and their wavering concerns began to fade,
fading until nobody was left to help me,
collect the fragmented pieces of my heart –
each time you broke it.

I remember just you and me,
no need for anyone new,
because you said forever.
I close my eyes, with your hands in mine
as I mouth the words "I love you".

My eyes are now opened, I see nothing.
Emptiness envelopes me, all consuming,
icy wind whips my fingertips,

And then I remember…that you left me too,
and I ask myself again and again but –
How could you?

Lost

I smile, finally feeling content.
But it's a clever game of deception played by my mind,
hiding me from the true state I am in.
Shattered. Broken.
Everywhere I look – I see you, I feel you,
always.
You have made my mind your humble home,
living freely in my thoughts.
Strong. Unmoving.
I am trying so hard, to slip past the fuzzy memories
of bellowing laughter and love-laced embraces,
but – I am failing.
And yet again, I am left questioning,
Will I ever find a love like yours?

If Only She Knew

Teeth white and glistening
as he smiled, palm outstretched,
she gladly met his hand with hers,
completing the warm embrace of
of two complete strangers.

If only she knew, as she stepped
into the unknown.
That this was the very moment,
she would live to regret.

Bad Habits

You are a drug.
Intoxicating and destructive at the same time,
so strong, it seems easy to overdose.
The highs with you, incomparable to
anything felt before,
but then, so are the lows.

Like Lovers Do

She could feel electricity
in anything he touched.
His words uncovered
eruptions of laughter,
so loud, it silenced
everything around her.

She had fallen for him.
for the sole reason that
he had made her believe in love.

Joker

Night or day,
either way –
you knew exactly how to play.
You held your cards right,
my game forever mediocre,
but little did I know,
you were trading with
a deck full of jokers.

Happy to See Me Hurting

You hid behind claims of insecurity,
angry and frustrated at my choice
to share my smile with the world.
Mocking my jokes and my heart.
I was open with you,
all my flaws and vulnerabilities,
only for you to use my own cries against me,
making me feel less than,
everything.

You built yourself up, by breaking me down,
so please tell me,
Are you happy now, to see me hurting?

Invisible

I noticed you,
Everything about you,
Detailed as each line decorating your palm.
Whilst you struggled to even see me.

Is That You?

It was as though
I was staring at you,
through frosted glass.
Face and shadowed silhouette,
foreign and faded.
Your actions silently vague,
increasing the growing distance
between us.

When you finally stepped
out from behind the pane,
your figure seemed
more blurred than ever.
The sad reality hit, bitterly true
standing there,
I barely recognised you.

Fading

In a world littered with billions,
the feeling of being alone is the most universally felt,
the emptiness, enough to consume you.
Darkness spreads throughout your entire
fabric until there is nothing left
for the lights' touch.

The search for any emotion is exhaustive,
constant waves of numbness,
shattered memories of your people-filled past
relentlessly tickle your mind like broken tides,
a flickering moment of bliss, suspended
in droplets of happiness.
You blink, now there is no one.

How quickly things change?
The faces of the ones you loved most
twist into that of a stranger,
names you swore would be with you for life
begin to fade into the abyss of the unknown.
Lost and fragmented.
Stabbing small talk about the weather and food
fuel the hopelessness.
The lack of purpose is all too much –
the blaze phrase "what's the point?" spat by a volatile teenager,
suddenly weighs so much more now.
The emptiness stabs your lifeless state daily,
persistent, deep, inescapable
yet, you still feel nothing.

Sweet Surrender

Is the fight really worth it?
Fighting for someone,
who, when given the chance
wounded you – again and again,
so heartlessly cold,
moving on quickly with the next troop.

Only to leave you there alone.
Bleeding and fallen,
riddled to the bone
with all the bullets,
you had taken for them.

It Was Too Late

She only cared because
she loved him.
She only cared because she
always wanted to see him smile.
She wanted to play happy,
within the safety of their glossy
bubble, shielding their unity from
the thorned-earth around them.
She cared, because even in a world
full of millions, she could
only ever see him.

So, why did he only care,
when she was gone?

Was It Real?

If you cared, would you
have led me on with glazed illusions
and love-infused promises?

If you cared, when things
twisted bitterly, would
you have hurt me the way you did,
with no interest for my pain?

If you cared, would you have left
me in the dark, just as a faceless
stranger would have?

My question is,
did you ever really care?

This Pain

You lit the match
and set me alight,
burning as a piece of paper would,
charcoal edges smoked
throughout my entire being.

Heated flakes cracked, breaking
away from me,
falling piece by piece, until
there was nothing left for you
to burn, the next time
you came with flames.

Stunted-Growth (I)

Planted seedlings of trust
into your pockets of soil,
giving them all – time, love and energy,
to allow the strong stalks of faith
to carry us through both,
calm and volatile weather.

I wanted us to grow together.
Yet, when the breeze got a little stronger
you ripped out the embedded shoots,
root by root.

Self-Growth (II)

Stunned, I stare at the
remaining seeds that had
not yet been sown,
gripping them tightly, precious,
glistening with hope.
Knowing now, that at least they
were safe to grow with me.

Tongue-Tied

Even though no words
swept through,
the void vastness between us.
We both somehow,
already knew.

50/50

The crust of the ground
beneath her, slowly splits apart.
Cracking the dry, earthy film
protecting the world,
feet on either side of the
moving fracture,
she stood torn.
Should she go back
or carry on forward.

No Caller ID

Someone I knew for years,
now calls through as a stranger would.
Unknown, twisted whispers
fill the empty space between us,
"I am not the one for you."

You leave, weighted with guilt
although it hurt, stuck in the static silence,
you had no idea how much
I needed to hear this.

Plot-Twist

You, the narrator of our journey,
carefully scripted, laced with
complex plots
of mistrust and deceit.

This show cannot go on.
Pulling the ropes
dust fills the air, a dissipating haze.

I let the curtains close
dividing us completely.
Finally, giving myself the chance to
write my own story.

Our Last Hello

I knew for a while now.
That this would be our last time,
of holding hands as we walked
down the cobbled pathways of the city
we both knew so well.

So, as I finally turned the corner,
I see the brightly spotted berry tree.
Our spot. I smile as I see you standing below,
running now, I embrace you tightly,
knowing already, this was our last hello.

It Hurt Me, to Hold On

I tried to hold on so tight,
to the point where, my hands were bruised
and my heart was weeping.
I just know, I should have let go years ago.

Two Hearts

Two hearts established a connection,
strong to touch, industrial upon the eyes.
Although it lacked the solid foundations
of trust and understanding,

Such a connection –
was bound to be weathered
by the cruel nature of time.

Act of Kindness

Held together by
pieces of splintering string,
through my glazed eyes I saw,
your tears mirrored my own.
I knew within me, through to my bone,
the most loving thing I could ever do
was to let you go.

Out of Touch

Never look back,
everyone forever bellows.
Since our strange rift,
I've never felt the
burning urge to turn around,
because what's the point,
when I know you, will not
be standing there, smiling,
waiting for me.

Other Side

I thought the trickling streams,
littered with rough stones,
would have been enough,
to stop you from crossing,
my love.

It seems, the stones
have steadied your feet,
allowing you to move on.
Seamlessly, over your puddles
of empty promises,
to the opposite side of the bank,
You are comfortable, as you take a seat,
rested under tiled, leafy canopies,
wrapped within the comfort of new company.

From afar, I see,
you're happy, you're free.
I guess it's true about the other side,
the grass really must be…
so much greener.

All I Have Left

The only version
I have left of you,
is one that is imprinted
within my mind.

Fleeting memories of
intertwined hands and shared coffee,
seemingly pale with each
passing second.
I just know my version of you,
is one I never want to lose.

Love to Hate

She slowly gathered
the wilted petals,
from the bright bouquet
you had once gifted her.

Love and Hate,
you somehow defined
both for her.

Your Name

Your name, was not on my mind,
nor, did it cross the rosy skin of my lips.
It remained an elusive word, outside
the strong barrier of my entangled thoughts.

But, no matter how hard I try to forget you,
I cannot deny that your name,
will be one that I always remember.

When the Sky Is Grey

Days like this,
surrounded by shallow grey skies,
I find myself back to the spot,
where we first met.
A time where I called you mine,
those moments so pure, almost magical.

Staring back at the ashy skyline,
the air now, seems a little lighter,
the clouds now silver and glistening,
just a little brighter.

Progress, Not Perfection

Today has been a good day,
my energy directed and focussed,
free to grow without the weight of compromise.
I feel lighter now, without you.

Rested for the silence of the night,
your smile and soft eyes infiltrate the darkness,
bursting the pockets of peace within my mind,
highlighted memories with you
flood the crevasses of each thought,
every cell clinging to your comfort.

I twist, diminishing my delusion.
Frustrated at myself for allowing
you back in once again,
But it's okay.
I sit alone, silent, as I remind myself,
that this is still progress.

Tidal

Tides rush out
of the body of blue,
ready to consume the
ever-spanning mass before it.

Yet, right before the tide
creeps up too high,
the waves lap and pull
the flow, straight back into
the limitless abyss.

This is the beauty of balance.

Protect Your Peace

Do not mistake the pain for love.
There is no healing in embracing
the blazing flames that burnt you,
just because you feel alone.

Too Comfortable

You lost your claim on me.
Every lie, every fake smile
only pushed me further away.
Yet you failed to notice,
just as you were blind to all my pain,
my sad days, the constant rain.
You never tried to understand
as you were too comfortable.

Under flicked eyeliner and bronzed eyeshadow,
there was me, the real me,
beautifully flawed, laced with tinted imperfections.
Forgiving you once was my biggest mistake,
But not again, with this I let go,
allowing you to fade into a stranger once more.
Erasing you from my present,
to free myself for the future.

I give myself everything you could not.
Alone within the depths of my own company
I breathe slowly and smile,
allowing myself to finally feel comfortable too.

She Is Art

My skin like bold lines,
arching and curving,
intertwining and mingling
at every joint and dip,
outlining the divine
canvas of my body.

You saw art.
You had a vision.
Held your collection
of fibrous brushes,
chose colours, gold, yellow, green,
splashed me with splatters
of happiness and love,
always colouring outside my lines,
abundant and overflowing.

Even after everything,
I stand here, alive and vibrant,
painted with every
lesson you have taught me.

Time-Lapse

Time serves us a test
that nobody can pass.
Flowers bloom eagerly,
only to wither away the next day.

Our skin flawless, fresh,
before being wrung through
the iron hands of the clock,
leaving us drooping and wrinkled.
Although, subtle smile lines and
scars, indent the lapsing hours
with endless meaning.

So please take care, to
always use your time wisely.

Drifting

Heavy ropes twist around
my bones, anchoring me down,
forcing me still – stagnant.

Cutting all ties,
I drift,
further and further away,
from familiar paths of pain
and well-travelled landscapes of
diminished worth.

Floating through crystalline waters,
this new scenery seems to be
complete, unexplored, bliss.

Note to Self

Let go of the things that break you,
now rather than later,
protect your heart as that is all you have.
Stop returning to the pain
or else, there will be nothing left of you to give.

Daydreams

Cracked roof tops and rusted pipes
fill the pane of
the rattling train window.

The sky forever an infinite plane
of bright blue,
specks of candyfloss cloudlets
litter this space above.
Just as you tint my thoughts,
from time to time,
leaving me momentarily lost,
within the depths of
what could have been.

The tracks creak, the train slows,
jolting me from reminiscent streams.
I hold onto the handles, palms tight,
glancing at the sunlit
doors about to open,
as I prepare myself,
for the next stop.

Boundaries

Brighter and better days are always ahead,
At least that's what they say,
so why not try, try to touch the light beyond.

Eager to learn the true beauty of self-love
and new-found independence,
learn to adjust your life to their absence,
than to break your boundaries to accommodate
for their lack of love.

The Healing

Wrapping myself up,
silver silk lacing my skin,
holding together
my cracked shell.
Encasing my being, within the
warm shelter of my woven cocoon.

I choose to make myself stronger,
day by day.

For the First Time

For the first time,
I feel whole.
No endless, empty
cavity centred within me.

For the first time,
I felt enough.
No longer waiting for your energy,
to elevate my own.

For the first time,
my own presence
completes me.

Alone.
I glow, bathed in opaline moonlight.

In This Moment

Laughter infects the
air around her.
In awe, she watches
pure souls dance intimately,
through cheerful jokes
and friendly admiration.

Tingling waves of warmth
elevate this joy,
the love sparkling, so vibrant,
that in this moment,
she cannot help
but smile with them too.

Her Vibe

She let the music
guide her,
potted plants and
pastel posters spin around
her infectious excitement.

Finally, she was dancing alone
to the liberating beat
of freedom.

Sunrise

The heat of the light's rays
caress my face,
dripping the fabric of my skin
in tinted honey.

As the sun rises, gifting life
to everything beneath,
I remain enveloped within this comfort
hoping, wherever you are,
that one day, you will feel this warmth too.

Wishing You Well

My thoughts conflicting, when
it comes to you.
Your name like sour candy,
my mind's illusion of you, sugared,
conscious of the reality, stale.

Even so, hidden under the blankets of pain,
I was taught to love,
and for that
I will always wish you well.

Made in the USA
Monee, IL
03 May 2026

49437793R00036